SPECIAL OFFER

Protect the Ones You Love Most:

- Free One-On-One Assessment
- Spend 15 minutes to make sure the ones you love most are protected
- Everyone who applies for an Assessment receives a free gift

4 WAYS TO REGISTER

Mobile Text
Send a text to **58885** with your name and email with the keyword **"Drawers"**

Voice
Call 866-603-3995 PIN # 148463

Web
Visit http://TheBestGiftisYourLastGift.com

QR Code

Praise For *The Best Gift is Your Last Gift*

The Best Gift is Your Last Gift is chock full of life-altering information. Dawn takes a difficult, often emotional topic, and boils it down into easy-to-understand language, using humor to keep things light. The step-by-step approach is a comprehensive, yet simple, way to plan your life affairs.

—Melissa A. Wick, Attorney at Law
Elder Law & Estate Planning, PC

I have felt firsthand the compounded pain of losing my father to cancer, and then other family members to the ravishes of a misunderstood estate. If only we'd had a better understanding of end-of-life events! Here, in *The Best Gift is Your Last Gift*, Dawn Pruchniak beautifully provides a simple solution to preserving what is truly most dear.

—Kimberley Schumacher, Author
My Letters to Amy: A Search for Generational Healing

If you'd asked me before I read this book, I would have said I'm all set . . . that my family is protected and provided for. I was wrong, and I'm starting with Drawer #1. Then I'm going to give this book to my parents, so they're sure they have everything in order too.

—John Buckley, Executive Director
Adult & Child Therapy Services
Class of 2015, Leadership Greater McHenry County

A great take on an uncomfortable topic, *The Best Gift is Your Last Gift* presents information you MUST know, whether you like it or not. Dawn offers clear, complete guidance, infused with a welcome lightheartedness that keeps you reading all the way through. I was inspired to start "organizing my drawers" immediately!

—Diane Strzelecki
Freelance Writer/Editor
Marketing/PR Coordinator, Algonquin Area Public Library District

Finally, a book designed for the average person to read, so everyone understands how important—and easy—it is to get your "Legacy" in order. The worksheets and examples provide the reader with everything they need to fill their wardrobes. I will definitely recommend this book to my clients and friends.

—Noel Baldwin, CPA, CFE
President, NBaldwin Company
Accounting, Tax, Fraud, Forensics

I've seen it happen so many times. Parents work years to help build close relationships between their children. Then one parent dies suddenly, without their affairs in order, and the consequent months of financial and legal headaches destroy their kids' relationships.

Thankfully, in *The Best Gift is Your Last Gift*, Dawn walks readers through everything we need to know, simple step by simple step. What other authors and professionals make overwhelming and intimidating, she makes fifth-grade do-able, engaging, and funny. She actually makes "getting affairs in order" painless!

Kudos to Dawn for creating such an easy-to-understand book! It's one that truly helps readers to protect our most valuable possession—our treasured family relationships.

—Deb Webber, Wealth Advisor

Dawn and I have served together at our church for years. I have great respect for Dawn, as she is one of the most intelligent and kind people I know. With a keen sense of humor and sophistication, she communicates some incredibly powerful truths in this book, truths that have changed my life, and my family's future.

As a pastor, I had the distinct privilege of officiating her first husband's funeral (it was my first). Tom was an amazing guy who was loved by everyone. Tom was so passionate about his family, but he overlooked one huge area that had multiple unintended consequences and prolonged the grief process.

As a pastor, I walked alongside Dawn as she grieved and wrestled through all of the struggles in the aftermath of Tom's death. She told me she was having to try and pay bills, get accounts switched into her name, struggled to receive death benefits from life insurances, and many other challenges. She said, "Every time I have to navigate this with a service provider or life insurance policy, it's like I have to keep reliving the pain of his death. It starts the grieving process all over again."

Those words shook me to my core. I'm married, we have four awesome kids, and I thought, *I don't ever want to put my wife and family through any part of an experience like Dawn's.*

Things in my life need to change immediately! As Dawn was going through this, she dispensed wisdom to my wife and me of all that she was learning. We asked her to walk alongside us so that we could prepare well to prevent any unnecessary pain for our loved ones.

Dawn helped us, with the strategies in this book, to prepare for the unexpected. My wife and I now feel completely prepared in the event something happens, because Our Legacy Wardrobe is in order. Now I'm encouraging my friends and family to do the same expeditiously.

Don't delay in putting Your Legacy Wardrobe in order! You never know when tragedy may strike you or your spouse, because tomorrow is not promised to any of us. Taking responsibility now is one of the most loving things you can do for your spouse and kids.

—Kurt Von Eschen, Worship Pastor,
Willow Creek Community Church – Crystal Lake

Dawn's book serves as a valuable tool in my work as a holistic wealth management advisor, because it is the one resource that dives deeply enough to address everything that the idea of "having your affairs in order" should actually include. *The Best Gift is Your Last Gift* covers the gamut: what to gather, how to keep data current and handy, choosing the right helpers, and more.

Through her book and her personalized coaching services, Dawn supplies a much-needed framework for how to identify and map out life's details now, while emotions are in check, so that essential business can be better accessed and understood when the unexpected strikes.

While no one can save a family from grief, those who get their drawers in order are setting up their loved ones for a more reassuring experience when the terrible shock of loss occurs.

As a coach, speaker, and author, Dawn has launched a legacy of her own, which will undoubtedly bless many, many families with the intangible gifts that come from living ready—a sense of clarity, intentionality, and long-term peace of mind.

—Noël Thelander, AAMS™
Wealth Management Advisor

You may feel overwhelmed and incompetent before you begin reading this book. Organizing your life's documents can be a daunting task. But as I read, I gradually experienced a shift to feeling empowered and directed. I encourage you to be brave and give yourself, and all your loved ones, the gift of living ready. It's well worth it.

—Jolayne White, LMFT
(Licensed Marriage Family Therapist)

The Best Gift is Your Last Gift is a very relatable and clear-cut look at how to organize your life affairs. It is an excellent resource for demystifying the estate planning process, and for helping people do the important stuff they need to achieve peace of mind.

Dawn weaves elements of her personal experiences into the narrative, illustrating the importance of each point she makes. This personable approach encourages people to bite the bullet and start answering the tough questions their loved ones may face in the future.

—Stacy Stusowski
The Law Offices of Stacy Stusowski, P.C.

The Best Gift is Your Last Gift:

Do You Know What's in Your Drawers?

How to Organize
Your Life Affairs
to Protect Those You Love Most

by Dawn Pruchniak
Family Affairs Specialist

Published by Prudence Partners LLC

www.PrudencePartners.com

The Best Gift is Your Last Gift: Do You Know What's in Your Drawers? How to Organize Your Life Affairs To Protect Those You Love Most

Published by Prudence Partners LLC
PO Box 1315
Crystal Lake, IL 60039

Printed in the United States of America.

Cover design and interior art by Reece Montgomery, Business Book Productions.

Library of Congress Control Number: 2017901948

Contents

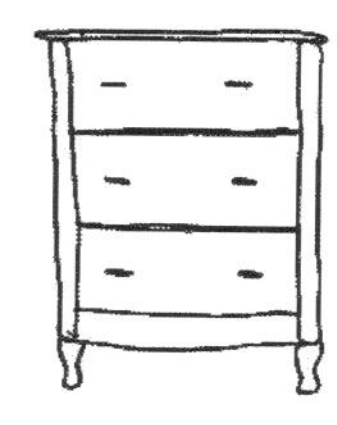

Acknowledgements

Thank you to all the professionals, family, and friends who helped me put all the pieces back together.

Janet Aldred
Marilyn Black
Karen Franzen
Mark Gerszewski
John W. Guanci III
Rich Pruchniak
Russ Robinson
Deb Webber
Jolayne White

The Best Gift is Your Last Gift

Dead Guys Just Can't Help

People hear "get your affairs in order," and they think, "It's too soon for the pearly gates!" They think gloomily of angels with harps. Of St. Peter handing out gilded You Are Here maps. They think, *The Big Good-bye*.

But "**affairs**" simply means "**documents that show what stuff you own**." (So **affairs** = **documents**.) And "getting them in order" just means "planning who your stuff will go to" since you can't take it with you.

The really great news is, getting it done is way easier than you've been led to believe.

At first, some people translate "get your affairs in order" into meaning they have to become financial planners—that they need to know how to purchase and sell stocks and bonds. Not at all! It simply means making decisions about the stuff you already own.

Why should *you* get your documents in order? I'll give you a hint. The reason isn't really about you. And it isn't about money. It's about protecting your family and belongings. It's about protecting your family relationships.

Why should *your spouse* get their documents in order? So that you and your kids will be protected if your spouse becomes the dead guy first.

Fact is, eighty percent of women die alone, as widows. That means 80 percent of men die married. That means, ladies, it's best to take care of this now, since you'll almost certainly have to at some point.

Here's a quick story.

In 2011, my husband, Tom, suddenly and unexpectedly died while our triplets were seniors in high school. Instantly I was thrust into getting all of our affairs in order. I'd had no idea how much work might be ahead of me if I lost my husband, or how much more terrible it would make the grieving process for our kids and me.

We Didn't Know What We Didn't Know

Tom and I had married shortly after his first wife had died. He'd been brilliant, funny, charming, but neither of us had been aware of what to update related to his affairs, including the paperwork that named his beneficiaries.

While scrambling to make funeral arrangements and wondering how I was going to support my kids as a single parent, I got a call regarding a surprise life insurance policy. The person said, "We need to know your mother- and father-in-law's address."

I thought, *Are they going to answer a questionnaire to see if I was a good enough daughter-in-law?* At that moment, that's where my head went. This person said that my husband had a life insurance policy, apparently one he'd completely forgotten about. I felt a teary breath of relief to hear it. But then I learned the rest of the details. Tom had taken out the policy roughly two decades earlier, when his first wife had been the beneficiary. After he and I had married, he'd never updated the information. His mom and dad were the second beneficiaries.

This person's goal was to give Tom's life insurance money to whoever he left it to, and that wasn't me.

At this point, obviously, Tom's first wife was dead. So was his dad. His mom was compromised, living in a senior care home. It was too late for the paperwork to be changed. And my husband's life insurance policy was going to go to my mother-in-law, and not to me to help support our kids?!

Eventually, after much heartache, that got resolved. But it happened to me again—two more times—that documents were incorrect. One of them was the 401k, because the form had been filled out wrong.

In all, it took months—I estimate more than **three hundred** dedicated hours—to get the documents corrected and to get my affairs in order. I had to do it all while grieving and helping my children with their grief. New problems kept coming up. I never knew when the stress was going to end. It was so easy to make mistakes on the forms!

For a year after my husband died, in addition to all the grief, I had angst over, "Who am I? What am I going to do? How do I go about deciding these things?" and, "How am I going to get through this?"

If Tom and I had known what a widow goes through to get her husband's affairs in order after he dies, we would have protected our family. We would have protected our financial stuff.

Life happens. But Tom and I hadn't lived ready.

You Can Live Ready

You can have both comfort and protection for family members who one day will be left behind when somebody becomes a dead guy.

People give three main reasons why they don't get their affairs in order: they're not old enough or sick enough, they don't have enough money, and they're too scared to think about it.

1. "I'm not old enough or sick enough." Do you know anyone who's waiting until they're old enough or sick enough to do anything? "I'm waiting until I'm old enough and sick enough to move to a beach house." No one has a bucket list for what they'll do when they're old enough or sick enough. When you're old or sick, or both, you're busy trying to survive.

2. *"I don't have enough money."* No one dies for free. Even if you die penniless, it'll cost someone. The dead guy's body has to be disposed of. Many people unknowingly place surprise financial burdens on their clean-up crews, their families.

3. *"I'm too scared to even think about it."* Please don't confuse grief with living in relief and peace of mind! Don't let your fear of grief prevent you from discovering how to manage your life without the dead guy.

Trust me, it's way less scary to think about getting your affairs in order *before* there's a dead guy than *after* there's a dead guy.

Scary is not having access to money in a bank account. Scary is not knowing when bills are due and if you have the means to pay them. Scary is wondering if you have enough money to stay in your home.

It's because people don't realize how problematic it is not to have their documents complete and correct, that so many people end up in a mess. It's why so many family relationships are forever shattered after someone dies.

You might think, *I have a will*. If you only have a will, the odds are your survivors won't be able to access the money until after probate—roughly a nine-month process. A will is far from ironclad!

That's why this matters. You can't help your family from the hereafter. But you can plan to help your family now, and quite easily.

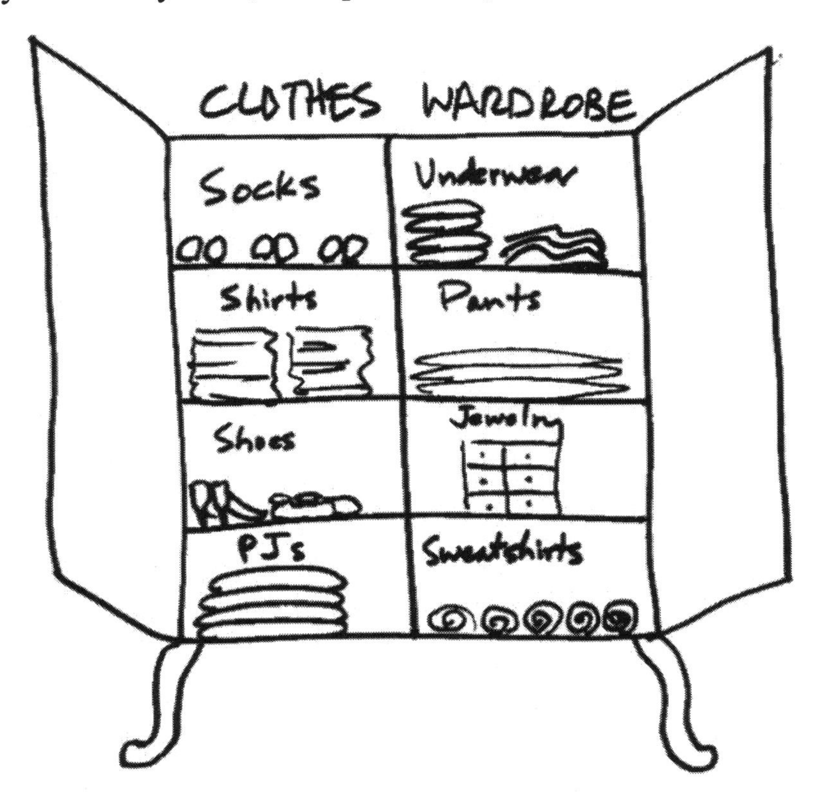

Your Legacy Wardrobe

"*Having* your affairs in order" means helping your family manage life well and continue their relationships when you become a dead guy.

That is the legacy you want to leave behind.

"*Getting* your affairs in order" means getting together your Legacy Wardrobe.

When you got dressed today, you found all of your clothes in an armoire, or a closet, or some combination. They were together in one general place, much of it likely in a piece of furniture. We'll call it a wardrobe. You didn't have to say, "I wonder where I put my shirt? I wonder if it's in the basement, the garage, or the backyard?" It was in your wardrobe.

That's how you can be with your **assets**. Your **stuff**. (**Assets = stuff**.) Or your and your spouse's stuff. You can put the documents related to your stuff into a Legacy Wardrobe—one specialized place.

When someone becomes a dead guy, how are you going to survive? How are your children going to survive? And how are the relationships going to survive? Because whoever the dead guy is, that person can't say, "This is where everything is. This is how you should spend the money. This is who's going to get what." Dead guys just can't help.

The emotional reality is that grieving, helping your family weather the loss, planning and paying for the funeral and burial, and paying all of the regular bills then and in the months that follow—all of these situations cause overwhelming angst. If you don't live ready, your family's future is uncertain. It's full of unknowns.

Turn Unknowns into Knowns

So what we're doing in the following pages is turning unknowns into knowns. We're ensuring a spouse and children will survive the loss of a dead guy as well as possible. Instead of leaving the family in angst, we're making sure they can manage their lives.

So let's put together your Legacy Wardrobe. It has only eight "drawers"—eight steps. The result of these eight drawers will be *five (5) actionable pieces of paper* and their supporting documents, and that will be everything you need to get your affairs in order. Voilà! Then you'll always be able to review your life affairs at a glance.

Now, the reason we wear clothes is for comfort and protection. The reason we create Legacy Wardrobes is the same—comfort and protection. We do it to comfort and protect our spouses, kids, and other loved ones.

Do you know what's in your drawers?

Let's start by locating your documents to find out!

LEGACY WARDROBE
1
2
3
4
5
6
7
8

Fact: Dead guys can't tell you where they filed stuff.

Does it really matter?

Dawn says:
Only if you want to keep living in your home.

Drawer #1

Discover What You Have & Where It Is

(Master List of Assets)

When you look into your closet or wardrobe, you see, “Okay. Three suits. Shirts. Pants. Five pairs of socks.” Because you’ve located it and you’ve organized it, you know what you have.

Your Legacy Wardrobe’s Drawer #1 is simply about locating important documents, so that you know what you have and where those important documents are.

What is an **important document**? It’s a document that proves you own something.

For example, your 401k, IRA, and life insurance each come with a document that shows it’s yours. (So **important document = shows ownership**.)

You need to locate these important documents in order to protect your family. How does locating these documents protect them? Because if you can’t find the documents that show ownership, then your family can't file claims or apply for benefits.

That would be bad.

Picture this. Your husband dies suddenly. He stops earning money (because dead guys can't earn money). So the money he would have earned, you no longer have. That means you need something that'll supplement your own income . . . or, you might not even have an income. If he has planned for you to keep living in the same manner you're accustomed to living, typically that's called a life insurance policy (or policies). That's *replacement income*. The life insurance policy replaces his income. This is what you're going to live on.

And the rule of thumb is the amount of the life insurance policy should be six to ten times his yearly pay. Then the survivor has money to replace the dead guy's income.

Unfortunately, sometimes there is no life insurance policy—one was never created in the first place—or the husband never had adequate life insurance. Sadly, this is why most widows live in poverty. It's why many of them can't keep living in the homes they shared with their husbands.

So life insurance policies are the things that determine the kind of lifestyle you'll have after someone becomes a dead guy. That's why they matter.

So for somebody thinking, *What the heck—documents? Who cares about that?* These kinds of documents determine if you'll continue living in the same lifestyle—and the same home!—you had when your spouse was alive.

However, no one wants to go on a hectic treasure hunt to find these important documents after someone becomes a dead guy.

Because, when somebody dies, the first thing you have to do is find out, "Where are their important documents? What stuff did they own? What properties, life insurance policies, IRAs?"

When my husband died, I didn't have that information. I didn't know, "Oh, I'm looking for ten things. Oh, I'm looking for three things." I had no idea how many things I was looking for. So, I had to go through tons of paperwork—every piece of paper we had from desk drawers, file cabinets, boxes in closets, the basement, the spare bedroom, the garage—*everything*, because I didn't know what stuff he had and didn't have. It was horrible!

So let's make it easy for you! Let's find your and your spouse's documents now.

This is a lot like inventorying your clothing wardrobe or closet, where you organize things by color, season, shirts, pants, suits. Then you can see what you have before you even get dressed.

Likewise, once you have all these documents, the rest of what follows in the pages ahead is very easy. You'll know exactly where all your important documents are located, which is incredibly important.

Because dead guys can't tell you where they filed stuff.

The Treasure Hunt

Ever wonder how many assets (stuff) you own that have a document showing ownership? Well, let's find out. And as we do, make a list of all of those things you own. We'll call it your Master List of Assets. Your list should be simple, just a page or so, maybe less.

Write neatly, because this is a list you're going to keep.

(By the way, putting this drawer together is the hardest part of the whole "getting your affairs in order" process by far, just so you know. But it makes everything else go smoothly.)

Again, the assets (stuff) you need to list are all those that come with a document that shows ownership:

- life insurance policies
- IRAs
- pensions
- 401k's
- real estate properties and mortgages
- investments, brokerage accounts: stocks, bonds
- bank accounts
- motor vehicles: car, motorcycle, boat, tractor, trailer, airplane

Once you locate an important document, fill out a line on your Master List of Assets:

Master List of Assets:

Banks, Insurances, Investments, Properties

Date:

Company Name/ Account Type	Account #	Telephone #	$ Amount	Beneficiary/ Titled To

After someone becomes a dead guy, the clean-up crew will need the Master List of Assets so that they can wrap up the dead guy's affairs.

Do You Own a Business?

If you or your spouse owns part or all of a business, those affairs need to be documented as well. Being a business owner without documentation and instructions for your survivors guarantees they will be in a long, possibly never-ending, nightmare.

So you need to have a succession plan. When you become a dead guy, someone will have to take over or close up shop after you are gone. Speak with your attorney to create a concrete plan.

Now do this:

1. Locate all documents showing ownership of the important stuff that you and/or your spouse own.
2. Copy the above Master List of Assets or request a full-size version at www.PrudencePartners.com.
3. Write the information from each ownership document onto your Master List of Assets. (We'll talk about beneficiaries shortly.)
4. Collect all of your documents showing ownership into one pile, and perhaps secure the pile with a rubber band. These are your

supporting documents. We'll get back to them in a while.

5. If you own part or all of a business, speak with your attorney to create a concrete succession plan.

When you're done, you'll have finished putting together your Legacy Wardrobe Drawer #1, your Master List of Assets!

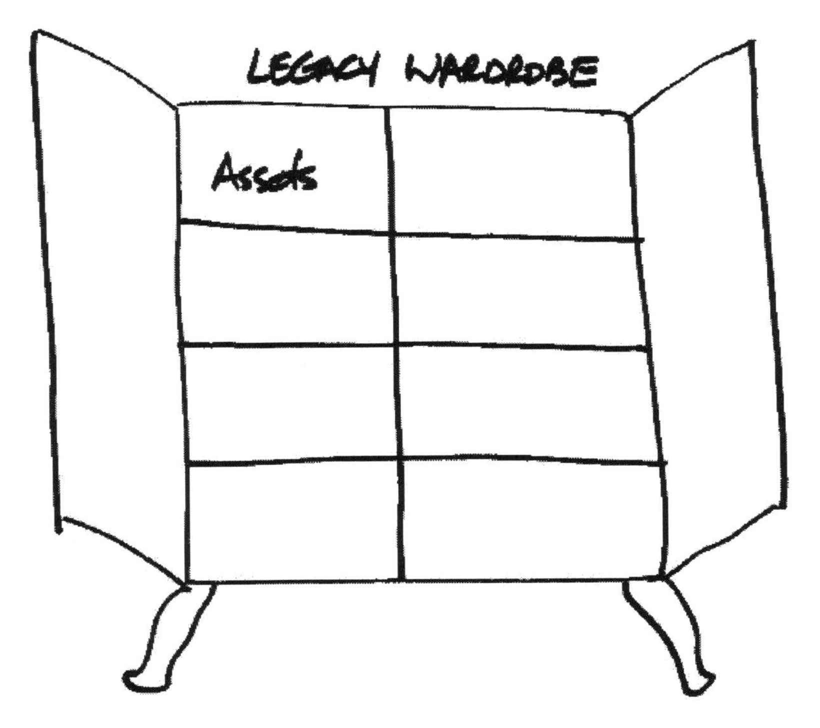

Coming up next: For Legacy Wardrobe Drawer #2, we'll make sure the money and stuff will actually go to the people *you* want them to go to!

You're on a roll!
Now let's discover how to fill in that Beneficiary column on your Master List of Assets!

Are you starting to understand that The Best Gift is Your Last Gift?

Fact: Dead guys can't fix mistakes.

Does it really matter?

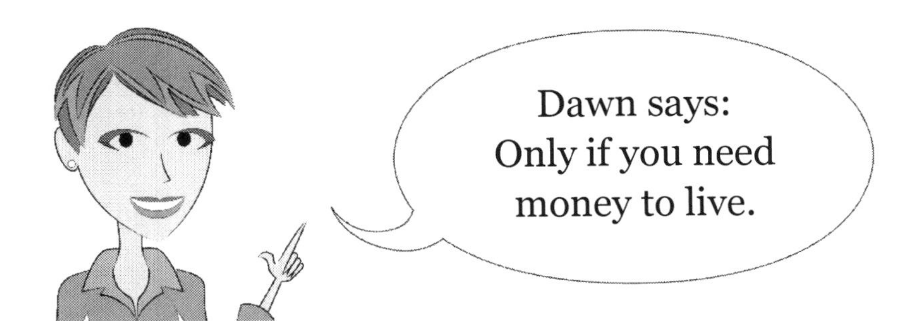

Drawer #2

Remove Unintended Consequences

(Beneficiaries)

For your Legacy Wardrobe Drawer #1, you made a Master List of Assets. So now you know *what* stuff you have.

For Drawer #2, you need to document *who* will get each of your assets when you or your spouse becomes a dead guy.

A person who gets an asset is called a **beneficiary**. (**Beneficiary = who gets a dead guy's stuff**.)

The document that reveals who gets what is called a **beneficiary form**.

Most assets (stuff) have their own beneficiary forms, which you fill out to name the beneficiaries. (You could choose to have one person get all the stuff. But who gets what is still individually spelled out.)

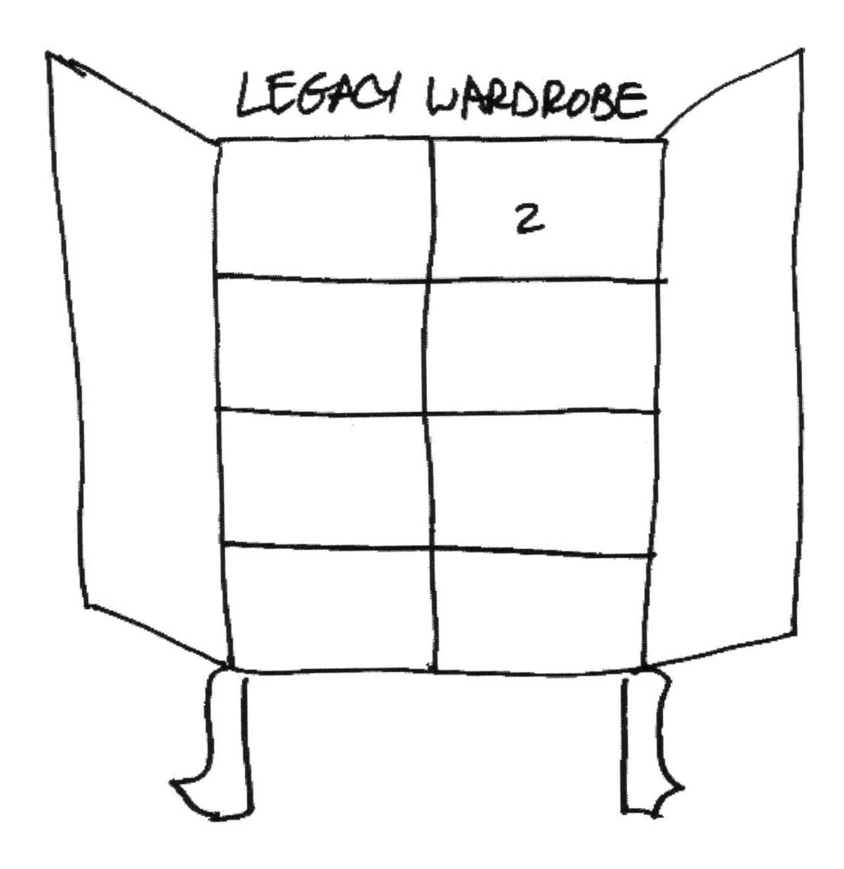

Unintended Consequences

I'll share with you that it's hard to think of anything more distressing than being a widow and not being listed as a beneficiary on your husband's documents. Tom and I had been married twenty-five years. We'd created a family together, built a life together. Yes, I received a phone call about a surprise life insurance policy, but I hadn't even been listed on it.

That wasn't the last memory I'd wanted to have of the husband I had loved.

Had my husband been alive, had somebody said, "Have you guys made sure your beneficiaries are right? Gee whiz, your first wife died—I wonder how many documents you have with her name on it," then my first year of living without Tom would have been totally different. I would have been able to grieve without also being forced to struggle while carrying a boulder of unnecessary stress.

But that was never a conversation between Tom and me. It was never even a thought. Had I heard what my first year as a widow would be like, we would have been on it! "Hey, we have to look at this!" It never occurred to us. We simply never thought about updating the beneficiaries.

Scenario—You're married, and you and your husband have kids. Your husband dies suddenly. Is your name on the mortgage? Will you get his 401k? His life insurance? Is your name on those? Are you the beneficiary?

Will you be able to financially take care of your kids and yourself after you've eaten all the condolence casseroles in your freezer?

No one willfully neglects beneficiary forms, but people who are uninformed often leave family chaos behind.

It strikes me as odd that beneficiary forms are often filled out casually, and in circumstances where that's not the main event. For example, someone gets a new job at a company that offers a life insurance benefit. The person goes to HR and fills out a hefty stack of forms about getting hired, taxes, health insurance, and other things. And somewhere in the stack of forms is the one about life insurance. Like all the other forms, the life insurance form has a lot of blank lines to fill in. And somewhere in the blur of blank lines is one that indicates "beneficiary." The person with the pen and the cramping hand is supposed to know how important that space is, what that space means, and fill it in correctly.

How do you make certain your forms are filled out correctly, with the right beneficiaries, so there are no mistakes? (Because dead guys can't fix mistakes!) If you like, I can help you personally. Simply visit www.TheBestGiftisYourLastGift.com.

Once you've made sure every asset has a beneficiary form—and that every form lists a beneficiary *and a secondary, or contingent*—collect all of your beneficiary forms together with your Master List of Assets, all in one place.

Ta-da! Then you'll have proof of whoever is the beneficiary of all the stuff.

You'll know you'll have money to live, while your dear departed bebops along glittering streets of gold.

Now do this:

1. Call each telephone number on your Master List of Assets.
2. Verify that the account name, the account number, and the business's telephone number are all correct. (Companies often get bought and sold and change names and numbers.)
3. Verify that the beneficiary is correct. If a beneficiary is incorrect (if you left an asset to icky Cousin Eddie instead of your current spouse), ask for a beneficiary change form so you can correct that.
4. Make a copy of your completed Master List of Assets. Put one copy on top of your pile of supporting documents, the one with the rubber band. Place the other copy in a folder. The folder will be your Legacy Wardrobe Drawer #8. Put the folder in a secure place.
5. Make sure everyone involved knows where the Drawer #8 folder is kept, as well as where you keep the supporting document pile with the rubber band.

When you're done, you'll have finished putting together your Legacy Wardrobe Drawer #2. Then you'll rest assured that your assets (stuff) will go to the people you want them to go to.

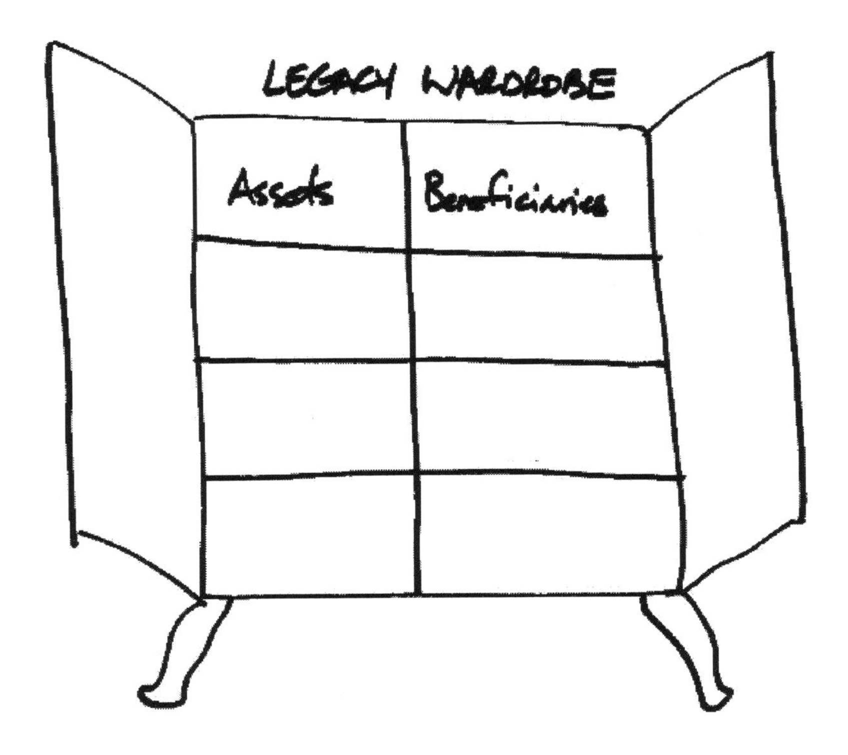

I'm remarried now. When I look at my and my new husband's Legacy Wardrobe, I think, *I'm okay. If my new husband dies today, I am okay. I know that. I have considerable, unbelievable peace of mind. I cannot control when he dies, but when it does happen, I have everything done.* I want the same for you.

New Stuff? New Beneficiary Form(s)!

From now on, whenever you open up a new account, an IRA, a 401k, a life insurance policy—just about any financial tool you could own in your life—fill in a beneficiary's name on the form.

Also, write the new stuff's information on your Master List of Assets.

Then place its supporting documents in your pile, the one with the rubber band.

Something Change? Update Your Beneficiary Forms!

Things change. Make sure to keep up with your beneficiary forms! Review them every three to five years or whenever a life change occurs, to be certain they're still accurate.

I call this a **beneficiary audit**. (**Audit** = **review**.)

What kind of life change?

- marriage
- divorce
- birth
- adoption
- change in health
- disability
- death
- geographical move
- job change

You refresh your clothing wardrobe more than once every five years, because things get out of date, or they don't fit, or they just look bad. Be just as dedicated to refreshing your Legacy Wardrobe.

That allows for best possible family relationships after you or your spouse becomes a dead guy.

Coming up next: For Legacy Wardrobe Drawer #3, I need to tell you why a **will** *won't do* what you might think it will do!

I'll also show you the nifty thing you can do instead! (Hint: It's called a **trust**, and you'll love what it does for you more than Spandex in your jeans!)

~ Best Gift Actionable Form 1 ~

Master List of Assets:

Banks, Insurances, Investments, Properties

Date:

Company Name/ Account Type	Account #	Telephone #	$ Amount	Beneficiary/ Titled To

Your first actionable piece of paper is complete! Now on to the second!

Fact: Dead guys can't write wills and trusts.

Does it really matter?

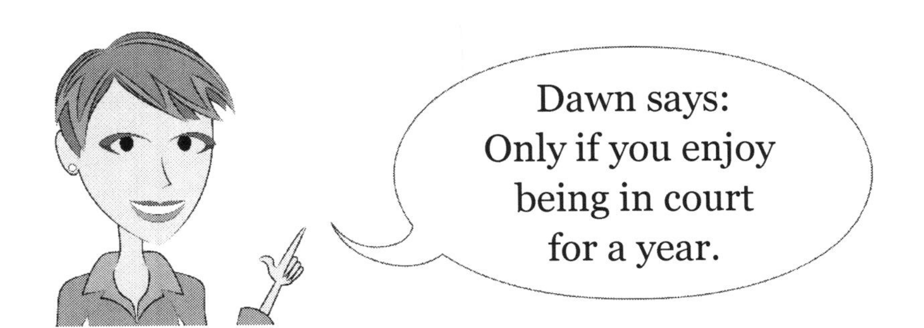

Drawer #3

A Will Is NOT What You Probably Think It Is

(Will & Trust)

If you read only one more chapter in this book, be sure it's this one. Wills and trusts—and lack of them—have the power to either destroy the relationships of survivors, or to protect them.

If you look at a will or a trust, it's a document. Maybe twenty pages thick.

Wills and trusts dispose of dead guys' assets. Their estates.

Whoa—estate?, you think? *I don't have enough money to have an estate.*

When I think of an estate, I think of somebody with more money than I can imagine. I picture they have a limo driver, a butler, they have maids, and that's what an estate is.

But the reality is that everybody has an estate, and when there's a dead guy, it has to be closed out. Why? Because the dead guy's house and stuff can't just sit where he left it, growing weeds and collecting dust until the end of time.

However, until people see why a will or trust is relevant to them, they don't get it. Here's why wills and trusts matter. If a dead guy has no will or trust, nothing speaks on his behalf regarding his stuff and who it goes to.

So a will or trust speaks on behalf of the dead person. It represents the dead guy's wishes and what and how he wants his stuff transferred to survivors. It also gives a designated person decision-making power to carry out those wishes.

If there is no will or trust, a judge will decide who gets what. And that is an expensive and lengthy legal process, the outcome of which is uncertain.

A will or trust is *that* important.

We put together the first two Legacy Wardrobe drawers in order to prepare for this one.

So, the will/trust is your Legacy Wardrobe Drawer #3.

As documents, wills and trusts have only a few pieces of information that are actually meaningful to you, the guy with the stuff:

1) Who's the **executor** or **trustee** (**the person in charge of distributing assets**)?

2) Who's getting the assets?

3) When?

(So **executor** or **trustee** = **the person in charge of distributing assets**.)

Too many people say, "Oh, I have a will, so I'm covered." And they're not, but they don't know it.

Other people say, "What's the difference? A will, a trust… It doesn't really make any difference."

Yeah, it really does make a difference. Unless you enjoy being in court for a year.

Following are the basic differences for estates that exceed $100K. If your estate is worth less than $100K, it will not go through probate.

Will	**Trust**
You *don't* have to list all of your assets in a will.	Your Master List of Assets *does* go into your trust.
A will is about property distribution after death.	A trust is about property management during your lifetime (very important if you become incapacitated) and after death.
Goes into effect after there's a dead guy.	Goes into effect when it is created.
There's *no* protection from creditors with a will.	There *is* protection from creditors if you have a trust.
Public proceeding, published in the newspaper.	Private proceeding, not published in the newspaper.
Your will must go through probate (confirmation of your will in *court*). Probate: • Can take nine months to a year.	Your trust does *not* go through probate. No probate: • Immediate. The executor/successor trustee needs only the death certificate to

• Your assets/finances can't be accessed until probate is done. • An attorney has to be paid for all that time. • Other things have to be paid for all that time: mortgage/ maintenance on the house, property taxes, utility bills . . . and you can't just sell the house and get that money. • Costs 3% to 5% of your estate's value! For example, if your estate is worth $200K, probate will cost an estimated $6-10K!	smoothly start executing affairs. • Your assets/finances can be accessed right away. • No probate means no cost for it to go into effect.

Here it is again, simplified, because I don't speak legalese or financialese. I speak survivorese.

Simple Comparison: Probate (Will) vs. Trust

Consideration	Probate (Will)	Trust
Function	Distributes your stuff after death	Manages your stuff now and after death
Goes into Effect	After death	Immediate
Access to Assets	9-12 months	Immediate
Process	Public	Private
Protection from Creditors	No	Yes
Cost	3-5% of Estate	None

A trust avoids probate entirely. On the other hand, if your estate is worth $100,000 or more, and you only have a will, then your estate most likely *will* go through probate.

That means during the entire probate process, until an estate's probate is finished, a live guy can't access any of the money to distribute it. It means for nine months to a year, some live guy has to pay an attorney, plus pay the dead guy's ongoing bills out of his own pocket—mortgage, gas, electric, maintenance, property taxes, and homeowner's insurance—and that one can be a problem. If a home is vacant for too long, the insurance companies won't want to insure a vacant home. Then if the home is damaged by a fire or wind or heavy rain or snow, the increasingly stressed live guy will have to pay to fix it.

When people say, "A will, a trust—Oh, it doesn't really matter," I think, *Really? You'd rather give an attorney thousands of dollars of your money (minimum)? You'd rather give an attorney that money instead of your survivors? Really?* But people just don't understand what is involved if they only have a will.

A generation or so ago, things weren't so complex. Because before the '70s, there weren't 401k's. There weren't IRAs. Maybe there was just a life insurance policy. Everybody had a pension. Drawer #1 didn't have much in it.

Now Drawer #1 has a lot more stuff in it.

Thirty, forty years ago, most people's estates weren't worth $100,000. So most people didn't go through probate. Today people have more money, and houses are worth much more money.

And that's why trusts are coming into vogue now.

The situation has changed, but the conversations haven't caught up. And that means more people are headed to probate who never had any idea that going to court was part of the deal of having a will! Because they thought, *Oh, I have a will. I'm good.*

They don't even know it, but they're headed to probate.

So a will means that once a guy is dead, it's going to cost some live guy money, and it's going to cost time—a lot of time. And it's not the easy solution that you thought it was.

So it's like saying, "I want you to fund my death *and* pay my bills for all the months you're going through probate."

What Exactly Is a Trust?

Okay, you might be thinking, *I can see why a will is NOT what I thought it was. But what exactly is a trust?*

A trust, which is always accompanied by a will, ensures that beneficiaries will inherit the quick and easy way rather than the long, hard way. The hard way is probate—only a will. The easy way is a trust and a will.

So with a trust, the executor/trustee can start making decisions immediately, as soon as they have the dead guy's death certificate.

You can start receiving money. You can start selling things. If you want to sell the house, you can. With a will, you can't.

A trust is like a bucket. All the assets go into it. Then the dead guy's successor trustee is basically handed the bucket and its contents. There you go. Distribute the funds and stuff per my instructions.

Mostly a trust is a structure that protects money from creditors and gives immediate decision-making authority to the successor trustee, so that the money can go to the beneficiaries according to the instructions.

Again, all that is needed is a death certificate. The death certificate is the key that powers a trust's "engine" of disbursement.

For example, if I want to claim my husband's life insurance, they have to have a death certificate before they say, "Okay, we believe you." But after they have a copy of the death certificate, my kids and I are provided for.

Once a guy is dead, it's too late for him or her to write a trust (at least not legibly). So that needs to happen now, while they are still a live guy.

(**Note:** Not 100 percent of the population needs a trust. Talk to an estate attorney to learn what's best for your situation.

The estate attorney who helps you create your trust will also help you create your will.

The attorney will also help you create your powers of attorney (POAs)—I'll tell you the few things you need to know about those in Drawer #4—and a HIPAA, the Health Insurance Portability and Accountability Act. I won't be discussing the HIPAA, but your attorney will help you with it. In short, it provides access to private medical information.)

"Are You Kidding Me? This Sounds Expensive! Lawyers?!"

Expensive compared to probate? The cost of creating these critical documents is exponentially less than probate. With these documents in place, money is saved, time is saved, and family relationships are protected. There is no comparison.

Watch Out for Legalese

There's often a big communications gap between the legal community and the consumer community. Certain lawyers help draft trusts, but the people who hire them don't speak legalese. Many words and concepts are so new to them that they might not grasp everything their lawyer is talking about.

As a result, you may have a trust created, but you might be unaware that you *have to title all of your assets into the trust*.

Creating a trust is completely different from **titling assets into a trust**, just like constructing a bucket is completely different from filling a bucket with valuables.

So a person gets a trust created, but it's completely useless because there's absolutely nothing in it. A lawyer creates a bucket, and hands you the bucket, but the bucket is empty.

Some lawyers don't help you to put your stuff into the bucket. Others do. Find out. Ask questions. Communicate.

Titling assets into a trust is not as fancy as it sounds. It's as simple as getting a form from your bank or brokerage firm. You just tell them that you want to change the name on your account to the name of your trust. They will know exactly what you are talking about, because they do this all the time.

Your estate attorney can also tell you how to do this.

Your Teammates: Tips for Picking the Attorney Who Can Best Create Your Trust

First, the attorney you pick has to be someone you're comfortable with, and that you trust. Often a husband picks and works with an attorney, but the wife never meets the person. She needs to, in case the husband becomes the first dead guy. The surviving wife will need an objective expert she can trust.

Ask each family member and friend who has had a trust created which attorney they recommend.

Second, the person you pick should be an *estate attorney*, and one who actually does *a lot of estates*.

Most law degrees require very few courses in estate planning. So just because somebody says, "Sure, I do estate planning," doesn't mean they're experts at estate planning! Their expertise could very well lie elsewhere.

It's the difference between going to a general doctor and going to a specialist. Your will and trust are custom documents. They must be crafted to meet your specific needs. An estate attorney will need to be able to advise you and help you to customize both the will and the trust.

Here's an important distinction between a general attorney and one who specializes in estate planning. All attorneys start with a boiler plate trust and then craft it to your needs. General attorneys may stick closer to the boiler plate and may not use the most updated wording. That can result in ambiguity, such as, "You as the trustee *may* give so-and-so *some* money." That's way different from saying, "You *shall* give so-and-so *this amount* of money *at this particular time*." The more specific the trust's wording is, the more controlled the outcome will be.

Also, an estate attorney has the ability to probe and ask questions that will customize the documents to precisely fit your circumstances. During his or her years in practice, he or she has seen what happens to families, good and bad, after a live guy becomes a dead guy.

So they have the best experience to tailor-fit documents to your specific needs.

A word about distribution of your stuff. It's critical that you and your lawyer talk through the distribution strategy you're considering. Let's say your plan is to leave $500,000 to each of your two children, whose ages are twenty-five and twenty-three. This means that if you became the dead guy today, they would each receive $500,000. Is that a good idea? Probably not. At those ages, these young adults are still getting established in their careers and work habits. A strategy to consider is leaving them each X percent at thirty years old, Y percent at forty years old, with the balance at fifty years old. The possibilities are endless.

After family members and friends have recommended some estate attorneys, interview a couple. You have to be comfortable with their personality and able to relate to them.

Simply, you need to like them and trust them.

Once you've chosen an estate attorney, have your trust created.

After your trust is created, *then be sure all assets are titled into it!* Have your estate attorney confirm that your assets are correctly titled into your trust. This is how you fill your bucket. You put all your assets in there.

The ideal situation is for your estate attorney, financial advisor, and accountant to work together to create the best solution for you.

As a Live Guy, You Are Your Own Trustee

Earlier, to keep things simple, I said **executor = the person in charge of distributing assets**. It's time to clarify that definition. An **executor** is the person you appoint to carry out the terms of your will (a female is an executrix).

The person who does the same thing, but with a trust, is called a **trustee**. A live guy who sets up a trust is his own trustee as long as he is alive. When he dies, or can't handle his affairs anymore, the person who takes over is the **successor trustee**.

So a **successor trustee** is the person in charge of making decisions when a live guy can no longer handle his affairs, or distributing assets from a trust when the live guy becomes a dead guy.

Your Teammates: Tips for Picking the Successor Executor or Trustee Who Can Best Disburse Your Assets

You need a person to distribute your assets, whether you do a will or a trust.

When somebody dies, all the executor/successor trustee needs to do is receive copies of the death certificate, and then he or she can start carrying out the dead guy's affairs and distributing stuff.

Who should you pick as your executor/successor trustee?

Well, who do you want in charge of your Legacy Wardrobe?

Have you ever said to your husband, your best friend, your sister-in-law, whoever, "Hey, I need some clothes. Please just go out and buy some. I don't really care how they fit or if they match—whatever you pick is fine with me." Nobody does that!

Most women won't even allow somebody else to set their Christmas table, or to choose what outfit they're going to wear on any given day. Most women certainly won't choose someone who doesn't have the skills needed to do the job.

For example, if icky Cousin Eddie is your successor trustee, and your beneficiaries are supposed to get, say, $500,000, and he's in charge, he could go spend it all. And the only thing your beneficiaries could do is sue him. The beneficiaries are stuck.

I know two people who had to drop out of school because the uncle blew all of the money, even though the money never belonged to him. He was only supposed to be the successor trustee, not the beneficiary.

So choose your executor/successor trustee with great care.

Being someone's executor/successor trustee is the worst job in the world. No kidding! Because it's that hard of a job.

People often think, *Oh, I'll pick my oldest child to be executor*. But that person may not have the skills. What other job would you select someone to perform based strictly on birth order? A surgeon?

Your executor/successor trustee may or may not be your spouse, or your mom, dad, adult child, sibling, or a long-time friend.

So here are some tips for picking a good executor/successor trustee. The person must:

- be trustworthy
- have excellent follow through
- excellent attention to detail
- good communication skills
- capacity to see a difficult task to completion
- ability to learn quickly
- emotional maturity so he or she will maintain objectivity, especially while working with the beneficiaries

The person who has those skills, and who you completely trust to carry out your wishes, should be the person you ask to be your executor/successor trustee.

When you create these documents, you'll also select your backup executor/successor trustee.

Will/Trust Master Form

Copy and fill out the following form so your key will/trust information is all in one place. Or, request a download for the full-size version at www.PrudencePartners.com. (We'll discuss POAs soon.)

Will/Trust/POAs Master Form for Spouse ____________ (name)
Executor/Trustee: Number:
Successor Executor/Successor Trustee: Number:
Estate Attorney: Number:
Accountant: Number:
Financial Planner: Number:
Employer: Number:
POA Health care 1: Number:
POA Health care 2: Number:
POA Finance 1: Number:
POA Finance 2: Number:

Next, identify key players—you, your spouse, children. Fill in the following information for each person.

	You	Spouse	Child 1	Child 2
Name				
Address				
Ph #				
DOB				
SSN				
E-mail				

Finally, write your distribution strategy.

Distribution Strategy
__% goes to __________ (person) at ____ (when).
__% goes to __________ (person) at ____ (when).
__% goes to __________ (person) at ____ (when).
__% goes to __________ (person) at ____ (when).

Now do this:

1. Pick a qualified estate attorney.
2. Pick an executor or successor trustee to manage your will or trust. Make sure they agree to be your executor or successor trustee.
3. Create your trust and will.
4. Title all of your assets and important documents into the trust.
5. Request a full-size Will/Trust/POA Master Form at www.PrudencePartners.com. Fill out the form, except for the POA information. (We'll discuss POAs shortly.) Or, complete the all-in-one Will/Trust/POA Master Form on the page that follows Drawer #4.
6. Put your will, trust, and related documents that your estate attorney helps you to create into your pile of supporting documents, the one with the rubber band.

7. Give your successor trustee a copy of your trust, in a sealed envelope, along with a copy of your Drawer #8 folder. Update every year. Make sure they know the location of your supporting documents—the pile with the rubber band.
8. Make sure your executor/successor trustee and POA agents know where the Drawer #8 folder is kept.

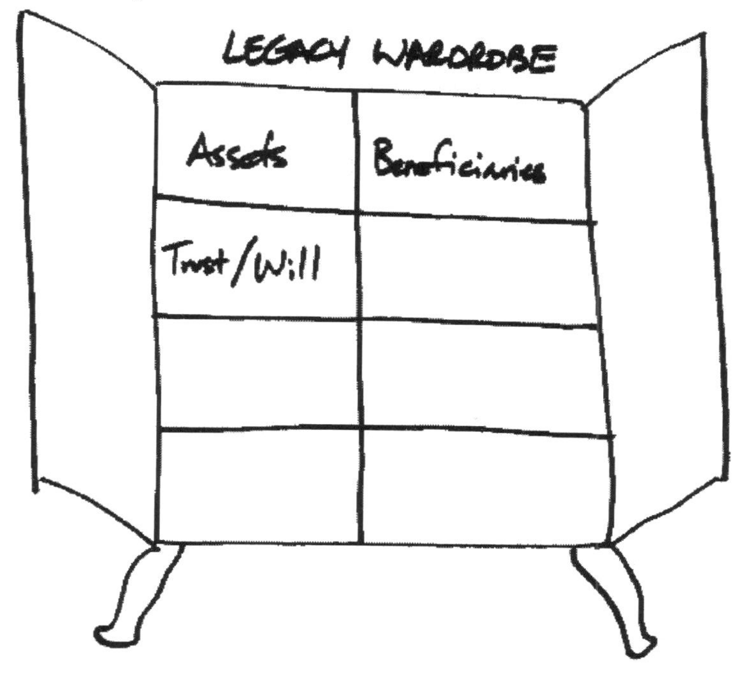

When you're done, your Legacy Wardrobe Drawer #3—*the most important drawer*—will be complete. Then you'll have complete confidence that the beneficiaries will be provided for, and your family's relationships will be protected.

Something Change? Update Your Trust!

Things change. Keep up with your trust! Review your affairs every three to five years or whenever a life change occurs to be certain your trust is still accurate.

What kind of life change?

- marriage
- divorce
- birth/adoption
- change in health
- disability
- significant change in personal circumstances
- significant change in personal financial circumstances
- change in assets
- change in tax laws
- death (including the death of an executor, successor trustee, or beneficiary!)
- geographical move
- job change

Keep your Legacy Wardrobe fresh.

Again, keeping up with changes allows for best possible relationships after someone becomes a dead guy.

Coming up next: Drawer #4 is the only drawer for *not*-dead-yet-guys! With Drawer #4, you'll learn how to get the health care treatment you want, even if you're too sick or injured to make decisions for yourself.

You're doing great!
Check out what's next!

Fact: Not-dead-yet guys can't make decisions about their health care.

Does it really matter?

Drawer #4

Who Speaks On Your Behalf?

(Power of Attorney for Health Care & Finance)

For some odd reason, some of our mothers told us to wear clean socks in case we're ever in an accident. "Take clean socks out of your drawer every day and put them on, just in case." (As if, while we're being pried out of a wrecked car with the Jaws of Life, the firemen will stop and pull off our shoes to check our socks for cleanness.) And *that's* the advice these well-meaning moms give for life's accidents?

But what if you're incapacitated? What if you're alive but unable to speak for yourself? How about what kind of medical testing and treatment you want to get?

Power of attorney (POA) documents give authority to someone to make decisions on your behalf if you're incapacitated.

Someone incapacitated can't make decisions about their health care, and they can't make decisions about money. A POA gives someone you trust the power to carry out *your* pre-documented, pre-communicated requests.

Most people have at least heard of POAs, and had the general concept floating around in their minds, but they haven't fully grasped how important it is that they themselves, and not some doctor or judge, decide what happens to them if they're an incapacitated not-dead-yet guy.

All the other Legacy Wardrobe drawers are for survivors of dead guys, about what can't be done or changed after death. This drawer can help to keep you alive, but it can't be filled after you've been rolled, unconscious, like a limp noodle, into the ER. So you have to fill it before you need it.

As always, I'll keep this short and easy! There are two kinds of POAs.

- A **POA for health care** (called slightly different things in different states) is about testing and treatment. (For instance, How much testing? How much treatment? Will you want a feeding tube? Would you want to linger in a state that you don't want? Maybe you would. That's everybody's personal decision. Do you want your life prolonged at any cost? Do you want it not prolonged at almost any cost? With a POA you're making a decision really easy for someone else to make on your behalf, because you've already told them, "These are my parameters." They're outlined in the POA document.)

- A **POA for finance** (also called different things in different states) is about managing money on your behalf, including costs related to your health care.

When you're alive, you can make decisions for yourself. When you're dead, you can't. But when you're incapacitated, we don't know which way it's going to go. That's what a POA does for your future.

The POA is your Legacy Wardrobe Drawer #4 (the one with clean socks).

POA—What You Need to Know

The How

You can download a POA document for free, but I usually don't recommend do-it-yourself legal or financial documents. You can work with an attorney to create a POA quite affordably, which I do recommend, and it doesn't take long. Then sign the POA, have it notarized, boom. You're in business.

Do your power of attorney for finance the same way.

Choose your attorney similar to how you chose one for Drawer #3. Ask each family member and friend who's had a POA created which attorney they recommend to do POAs. Then interview a couple of the attorneys. Make sure you're comfortable with them and can relate to them. Make sure they take time to clearly explain information, options, and what the options mean.

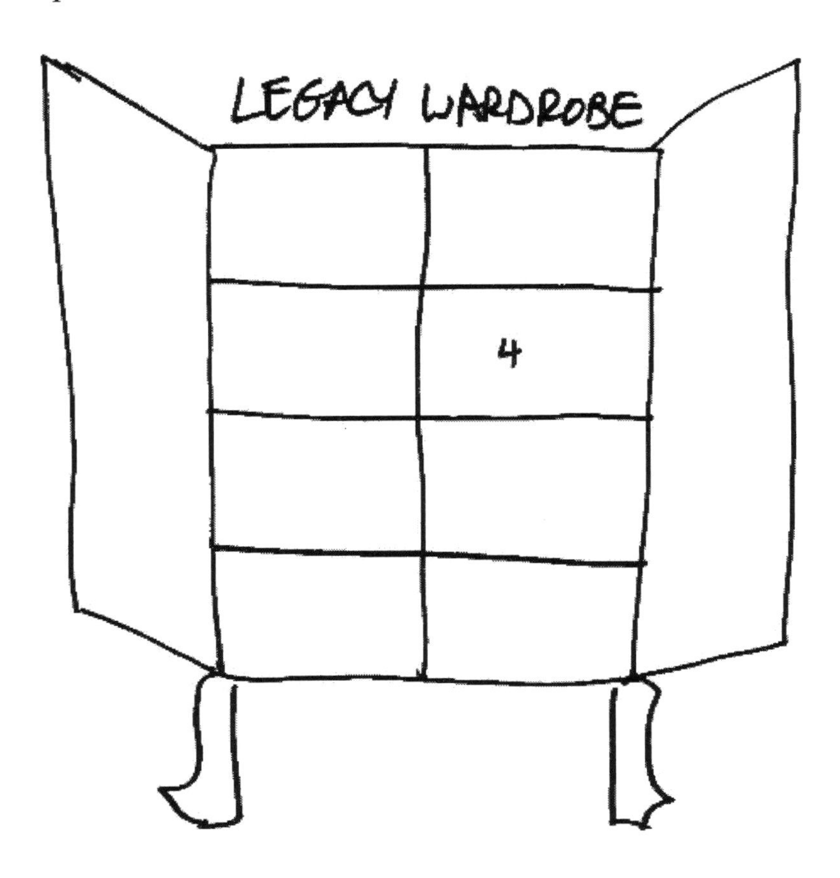

The Who

Who should you choose to be your power of attorney for your health decisions? Consider this. Will that be the same person as, or will they work in partnership with, your power of attorney for finance? Think about what relationship those two people have, and how well they'll work together on your behalf.

Could you ask one person to do both? Yes, absolutely. It depends on, Who is that person? Will they carry out your health care wishes? Are they good with money?

Maybe you want two people, someone who's got the heart to carry out your decisions to do the health care . . . or maybe you don't. Because if they're too soft and can't honor the decision that you've made, then you don't want that person!

Your POA for health care will need to abide by your wishes. And they'll need to work with your POA for finance guy who's going to decide whether to pay for those tests and treatments.

"I'm her son as well as her POA for health care, and I want my mom to have this experimental treatment. Oh, it's going to cost $200,000? Well, I can't make that decision. Let me ask her POA for finances." Then the POA for finances has to make that decision. In terms of your whole estate, can you afford it? Is it going to come out of his pocket? Will they not want to spend the money if it reduces his inheritance? Do they have access to that money?

Your POA(s) could be any adult family member or friend you trust to make those significant decisions. Ask the person you want if they'd be willing. When you've decided, let that person know that they are your stand-in, your POA person. Have a conversation about what your testing and treatment wishes are. Be as specific as you can. Write your wishes down if they aren't already spelled out specifically in your POA document.

The Where

After you have a POA person and a notarized POA document, you'll want a few copies. Give one to the medical center, if you're able.

Give another copy to your POA person or people. Because when you end up in the hospital, obviously you can't go home and retrieve the document to give to your power of attorney guy. They actually need to have the document, so that when they need to be your power of attorney for health care, that's their legal authority. That's what they show to the doctor and say, "This is what proves I have the decision-making ability on her behalf. Because she's in a coma."

Otherwise the doctor can say, "Why should I do the tests and treatment you want? You have no legal authority. I'm going to do the tests and treatment I see fit."

Note: Each state requires its own POA for health care. So if you live in Illinois but winter in Florida, the Illinois POA isn't valid in Florida. You also need a Florida POA for health care.

The When

Now that you have a better idea of, "Oh, *that's* why this is important," you might be wondering, *When should a person get a POA for health care?*

Anybody who's over eighteen years old should have a notarized POA document. If someone is over eighteen and married, their spouse could be their designated POA person.

If you're a guardian, mom, or dad, then as soon as you have a child who is eighteen years old, you no longer have authority to make decisions on their behalf if they become incapacitated, if they don't have a POA document that names you as their designated POA person. A doctor or judge could make decisions for your adult son or daughter instead. The family has no legal authority.

What actually happens will be dependent upon the personality of the doctor. The family's wishes may be considered, but legally they have zero authority to make a decision.

You have to have the document in place, or you might get no say.

Most people don't know that. So when your son or daughter turns eighteen, be sure to get them a POA for health care. Think birthday gift or Christmas gift. :)

You should get your own POAs now.

How Often

In only ten years, two people I had assigned to be my POAs moved. One moved halfway across the country, and we fell out of touch.

Update your POAs to name new decision makers as needed.

Not-dead-yet guys can't make decisions about their health care. So get a POA right away . . . unless you really don't mind staying in a coma. While wearing dirty socks.

Now do this:

1. Work with an attorney to create POAs for health care and finance, for you, your spouse, and your adult kids. (Anybody who's over eighteen years old should have a POA.)
2. Be sure to have your POA documents notarized, or else they're meaningless!
3. For the person(s) you choose to be your POA, you want to 1) remind them that they are your

POA person(s), and 2) give them a copy of the POA document(s) they'll need.

4. Fill in the POA information on the Will/Trust/POA Master Form you created for Drawer #3. Or, complete the all in-one Will/Trust/POA Master Form on the page that follows this drawer. Put it into your Legacy Wardrobe Drawer #8 folder.
5. Put notarized copies of your POA documents into your pile of supporting documents, the one with the rubber band.
6. Make sure everyone involved knows where the Drawer #8 folder is kept.

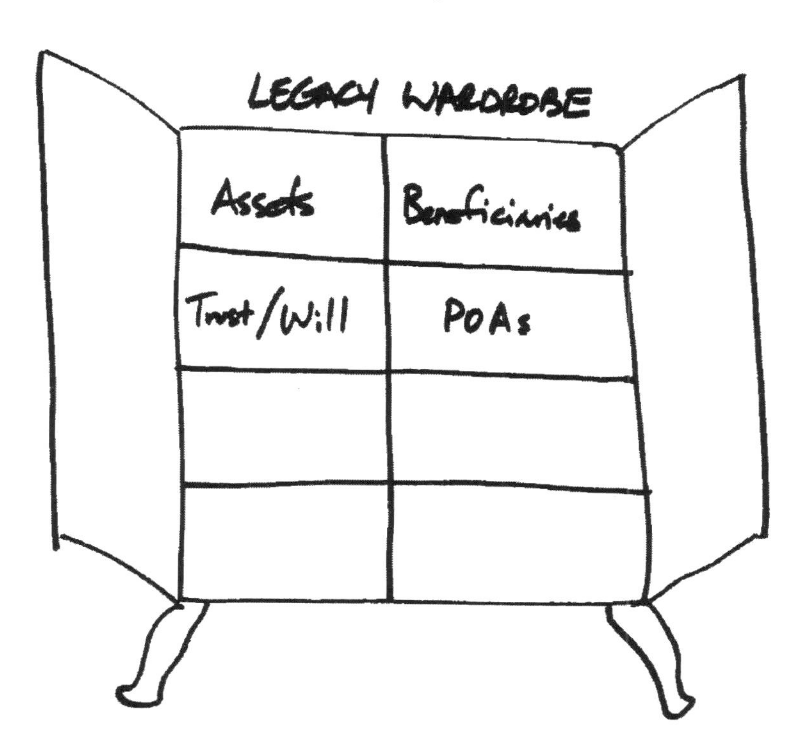

When you're done, your Legacy Wardrobe Drawer #4 will be all ready for those not-dead-yet moments. You and your family will be confident that good decisions will be made on your behalf, and that what you want is what will happen.

Coming up next: For Legacy Wardrobe Drawer #5, I'll show you how to avoid digital ambush—*and* identity theft of your spouse's information—for when your spouse dies.

Remember, The Best Gift is Your Last Gift.

~ Best Gift Actionable Form 2 ~

Will/Trust/POAs Master Form **for Spouse ____________ (name)**
Executor/Trustee: Number:
Successor Executor/Successor Trustee: Number:
Estate Attorney: Number:
Accountant: Number:
Financial Planner: Number:
Employer: Number:
POA Health care 1: Number:
POA Health care 2: Number:
POA Finance 1: Number:
POA Finance 2: Number:

	You	**Spouse**	**Child 1**	**Child 2**
Name				
Address				
Ph #				
DOB				
SSN				
E-mail				

Distribution Strategy
__% goes to ___________ (person) at ____ (when).
__% goes to ___________ (person) at ____ (when).
__% goes to ___________ (person) at ____ (when).
__% goes to ___________ (person) at ____ (when).

Your second actionable piece of paper is complete! Now on to the third!

Fact: Dead guys can't pay bills online.

Does it really matter?

Drawer #5

Escape Digital Chaos

(Master List of User IDs and Passwords)

When someone becomes a dead guy, they become an open target for identity theft and identity fraud.

People who are really good at that breeze through the obits daily, thinking, *Oh, so-and-so just died. I wonder if we can get their identity?* And then you have a mess on your hands, one that could take years to clean up.

For your Legacy Wardrobe Drawer #5, I'll show you how to easily prevent digital chaos and lockout from the dead guy's accounts.

Our digital identities are a huge, complex concern. If your husband dies and he was the bill payer, and you don't know his passwords—or if his hundred or more passwords are "organized" on notebook paper with dozens of old passwords scratched out and arrowed over to newer ones—then you can't get into his computer accounts. Maybe you can't even get into his computer.

You're not only *not* paying bills, you don't even know *that* you're not paying bills. You're not doing it on purpose. You just don't know that the bills are coming in.

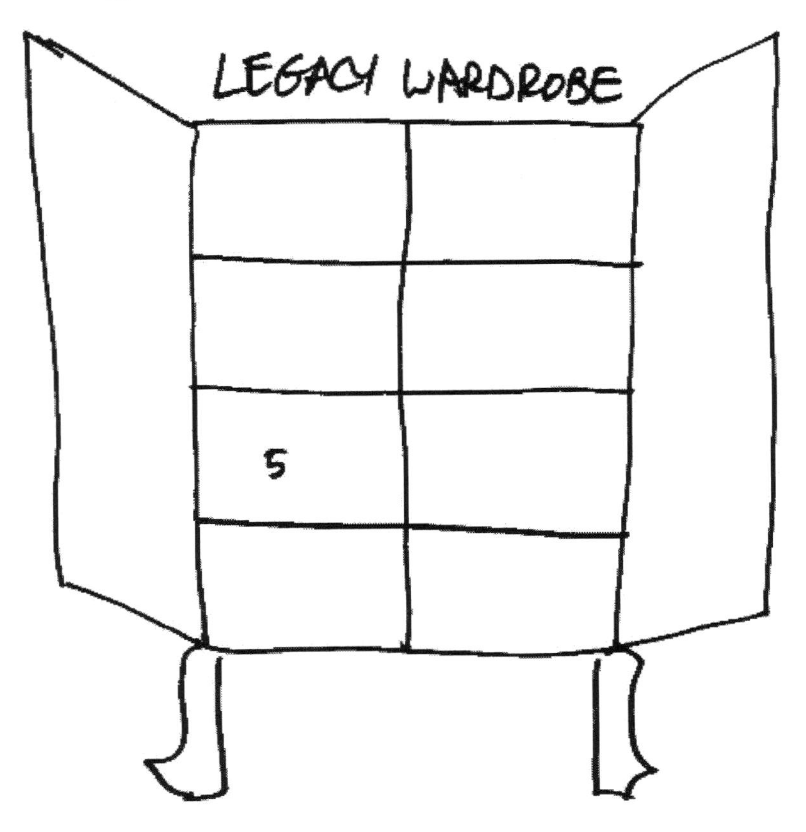

I have a new friend who's a financial planner, and she and her husband are really savvy about their Legacy Wardrobe. They update their affairs every year, and hand them off in an envelope to the person who'll manage things in the event of their deaths. After I chatted with her about the Legacy Wardrobe, she said, "I don't have any of my husband's user IDs or passwords." She knows Drawer #1, she knows Drawer #2, and she knows Drawers #3 and #4. Her Drawer #5 was empty.

So you want to be sure to quickly clean up your family's current system of digital records, because dead guys can't pay bills online. If the electric bill isn't paid, and if the water bill isn't paid, then your washing machine will be dead in the water, so to speak. And you won't have clean underwear.

You also won't have online access and security.

That means both spouses need each other's digital access.

Some Companies Are Like Dark-Humor Sitcoms

There's always a division of labor in a relationship, where you know some stuff, and your spouse knows the other stuff.

Well, if your husband is the dead guy, and he hasn't communicated how to locate his user IDs and passwords, or the password(s) to get into his computer, then *nightmare*! Many companies aren't set up for good death practices. That's not their primary business focus. It can feel like a slap in the face when you make one of those calls.

For instance, I met a gentleman in my grief group whose wife had been the bill payer. He had to make the phone call to the electric company. "I need to put this account in my name, because my wife has died."

They replied, "Well, we can do that, but we need a security deposit." Basically that meant, "Sir, for thirty years we've been doing business with you, but that was in your wife's name, and we don't really know anything about you. And if you're going to use our services, we need a security deposit—even if you're overwhelmed, in grief, and have to come up with the money to pay for an unexpected funeral."

The way they treat the survivor can be so insensitive, you can't even believe it! A lot of companies, how they operate, you think they must be writing material for *Saturday Night Live*. It's as if they can't have actually thought this through and be serious.

And that's just one of the kinds of things that happens!

You want to be in charge so that you can be confident. But you can't be in charge of anything if you don't have digital access to the other half of your life that somebody else is doing.

So you want to have access to all e-mail accounts, bill-paying, social media, and all other digital accounts.

Create Your Digital Master List

Maybe you or your spouse already has a Master List of User IDs and Passwords (it's important, so I capitalize it) on all of your accounts. I started doing that after my husband died, so there's a sheet of paper on my desk next to my computer, but it's ridiculous. There's a hundred, hundred twenty . . . I don't even count them anymore, but I keep making the fonts of the user IDs and passwords teenier and teenier so I can get them all on one page. But if the survivor doesn't have access to that, it's a nightmare to figure all that stuff out.

And while you're sorting through it all, you could be digitally ambushed.

Here's how to avoid that.

Rather than use pieces of paper or a notebook to make a Master List of User IDs (sometimes websites require both an e-mail address and a user ID) and Passwords, perhaps list them on a spreadsheet and print them out. Be sure to back up a copy on an external hard drive that can't be hacked.

Whatever way of organizing works best for you, remember to list the related e-mail addresses, user IDs, and passwords for all of your digital accounts.

- personal URLs/websites, personal blog sites, e-mail accounts
- mortgage payments
- car payments
- utilities—electric, gas, water/sewer, trash/recycle
- insurance—health, auto, homeowner's
- online statements/online banking
- credit cards
- loans
- investments
- PayPal
- autopay donations—such as church or charities
- video streaming services—such as Amazon Prime, Netflix, Hulu
- music streaming and radio services—such as Pandora, iTunes, Play Music
- newspaper delivery, magazine subscriptions, and other media services
- any recurring service—such as landscaping services, security services for your computer (Norton, Mozy), cell phone service, landline, cable
- social media sites—such as Facebook, Twitter, Pinterest, LinkedIn, Snapchat, Skype
- Dropbox
- Ebyte

- your network security key
- in-home network equipment
- I-PASS/electronic toll collection
- FAFSA information—if you've got college-age kids
- Social Security Administration and other government accounts

Can you imagine if you don't even know about your spouse's autopay arrangements? And money is coming out of your whatever account? A Master List of User IDs and Passwords puts you in charge.

A lot of people might already have a collection of User IDs and passwords, but they might keep it in different locations. They might keep their banking passwords in their banking folders, and they might keep their credit card passwords in their credit card folders. This way everything is all in one place.

On the last page of this Drawer is a Master List of User IDs and Passwords form you can copy and fill out. Or, you can request a full-size version at www.PrudencePartners.com.

Once you've created your Master List of User IDs and Passwords, keep updating it every time you sign up for something new or buy something through somebody online. Having such an easy to use Master List is a luxury even while you're an alive guy.

And if you do this before somebody's dead, then you'll have access to everything you need.

As another option, you could do some quick homework to find a service that will keep all of your user IDs and passwords in one place for you, such as Norton Identity Safe. Then you would just need one user ID and password to get into that service.

In the Event of a Dead Guy

When somebody dies, one of the first things to do is order twenty death certificates, because it's cheaper to place an order for more, all at once. If you run out and need more, they're more expensive.

Send a death certificate to each of the three major credit bureaus, and one to Social Security. That alone shuts down a lot of avenues for identity theft and fraud, so much so that it's unbelievable.

To request the addresses to the three major credit bureaus, visit www.PrudencePartners.com.

I have a relationship with two dead women I've never met. My first husband's first wife, who has been dead for more than thirty years—I still get her mail—and my second husband's dead wife. Still get her mail. Do you know how much mail comes in for Tom? Practically none. Because I sent Tom's death certificates to the major credit bureaus. And I didn't have a problem with identity theft or fraud.

Second, use the Master List of User IDs and Passwords to access accounts, pay bills, shut off autopay things that are no longer necessary, and close the accounts you want closed.

Now do this:

1. Create your household Master List of User IDs and Passwords.
2. Keep updating your list every time you sign up for something new, buy something through somebody online, or change a password.
3. Make sure the executor/successor trustee knows where the Master List of User IDs and Passwords is kept.
4. Make a copy and put it into your Legacy Wardrobe Drawer #8 folder. Keep the folder in a secure place.
5. Make sure everyone involved knows where the Drawer #8 folder is kept.

When you're done, your Legacy Wardrobe Drawer #5 will be good to go. The survivor and family will have digital peace of mind—and clean underwear—in the event of a dead guy.

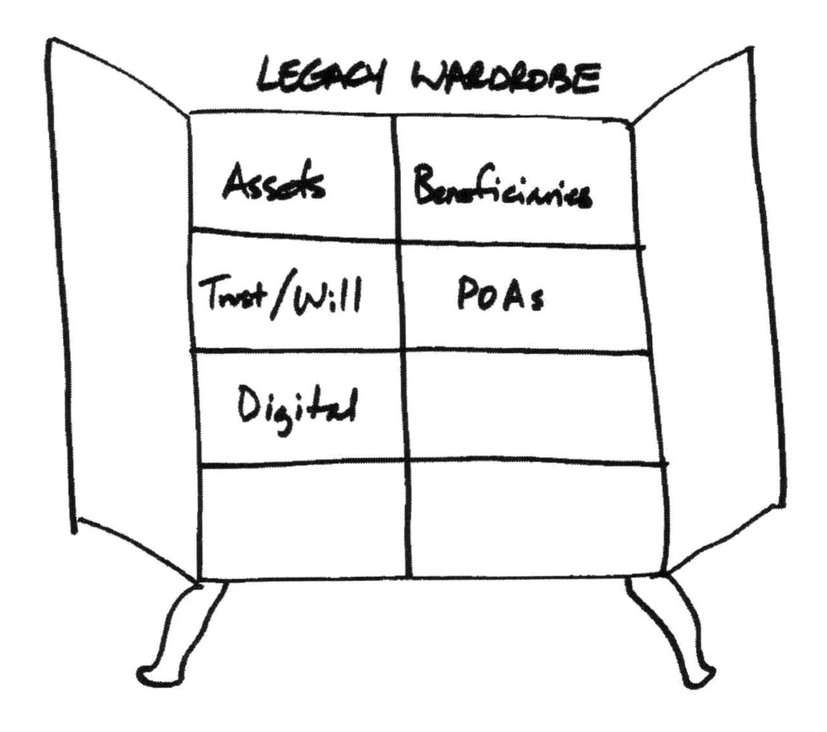

Coming up next: What if your spouse becomes a dead guy? What if you do? For Legacy Wardrobe Drawer #6, we'll set up a Yearly Conversation that will help you and your spouse plan for the living guy to manage well . . . so that neither of you ever has to fear surviving.

~ Best Gift Actionable Form 3 ~

Master List of User IDs and Passwords

Account/URL	E-mail	User ID	Password	Account #

Your third actionable piece of paper is complete! Now on to the fourth!

Fact: Dead guys can’t help you plan.

Does it really matter?

Drawer #6

Ready to Survive Alone?

(The Yearly Conversation)

When my husband died, I was charged with getting our affairs in order. And I thought, *Boy, if I could have even just one five-minute conversation with my husband . . .*

That conversation would have been filled with things like, "How many bank accounts? What's the password to this? Let's strategize. Do you think I should sell the house?"

That conversation would have been filled with all business.

I might have started with, "I miss you," but my very next words would have been, "Let's get down to business," because a widow is faced with running the business of her life without her husband.

Or a child is faced with running the business of your life without you to inform them, and they don't know any of the things that they have to know in order to settle your affairs.

Or if you are a business owner, your spouse or children will be faced with running or selling a business.

If your husband dies, how long will you be able to live in your house? When will you be able to afford a new car? How will you live your life? Will you live your life in a manner that you're accustomed to?

What will happen to you if he is the first dead guy? What will happen to him if you're the first dead guy?

The goal with Legacy Wardrobe Drawer #6 is to have a what-if strategizing conversation with your spouse yearly, so that the living guy is well-prepared to survive alone. Because dead guys don't wear thinking caps, and dead guys can't help you plan.

The Yearly Conversation (capitalized = important) is the big piece that makes all the previous pieces of your Legacy Wardrobe fit together. If you don't have this conversation, you are operating in the dark. In angst. Without this, you won't be living ready.

The Yearly Conversation—It's All about Future Decisions

Women freak out if an item of clothing they want to wear out to dinner is buried in the laundry pile. "Oh, your dress? You wanted to wear that tonight? Sorry, hon. I didn't wash it." But a woman doesn't give a first thought about what will happen to her if her husband keels over into his prime rib an hour later.

So have the Yearly Conversation now. When one of you becomes a dead guy, the survivor will be able to avoid freaking out about their future.

When you and your spouse sit down with pen and paper to make future decisions, also have 1) a budget and 2) a projected income if one of you becomes a dead guy. That's what helps you have a conversation.

If you don't know those two things, it's almost impossible to have this conversation.

With those in hand, here are some questions you should ask and ideas you should give thought to.

- "If you're the dead guy today, what will my income be? Do I have enough money to live on? Will I be able to live my new life in the manner that I am accustomed to? Or will I literally go into poverty? What changes in lifestyle will I have to make in order to pay my bills, based on my new income?"
- "Will I have enough life insurance as replacement income to live as I do now? If so, what do you think I should do with the insurance money?" Hopefully you work with an astute financial planner. It would be wise for the three of you to have this conversation.
- "If you're the dead guy today, do you recommend that I stay in the house or sell the house? And if so, for how long or when? Should I refinance the home?"
- "Will I have to start liquidating assets?"
- "Will I have to get rid of a car right away?" Or, "When will I be able to afford a new car?"
- If you're insured under your husband's health insurance, ask, "What should I do for health insurance if you're gone?"

- "Who am I going to feel safe with in your absence, talking about money?" If you don't currently work with a financial planner, it's a good idea to consider finding one now. If your family has one but you don't know that person or attend the meetings, you should attend the meetings. If you're a new widow in that not-knowing position, you need to trust somebody, but you won't know who to trust if you haven't met your financial planner. And when you're in a vulnerable place, people may take advantage of you, even if they're family members. So be sure you'll feel safe talking with your financial planner in the dead guy's absence.

If the husband's been managing all of those things, then he's been working those numbers in his head. He'll be able to say, "Our investments are such that they'll provide a steady income of $__ per month." Or, "This'll be worth this, and this'll be worth that."

And if a woman isn't used to thinking about that stuff, then she's left completely clueless. And she still may be clueless during the first Yearly Conversation, but at least a husband and wife can talk about, "Yep, if he was the dead guy today, then her income will be this much. Social Security, pension will be that much.

This is what you're going to be living on, and these are what your expenses will be."

As you outline your current budget and your projected income when one of you becomes a dead guy, you'll be able to see how the budget and income will work together.

The Yearly Conversation prepares you to financially manage life without your partner. At least the conversation enables you to *get started* living on your own, because you solicited an opinion from your trusted partner when you could.

It's a good idea for every couple, at least annually, to have this conversation.

Why have your what-if conversation yearly? Why keep updating your documented decisions? Simply because income and expenses change.

Because you won't have to guess when you know. Your Legacy Wardrobe will be completely organized!

A woman will know ahead of time, way before something happens, "Whew! I can stay in the house. And I can get those kitchen cabinets. I can even get that facelift." Or, "I might need to take my lifestyle down a notch, but I'll be fine. I'll be able to survive alone."

Every year, have the conversation and document your updates. "Oh, the kids are out of college now, so I don't have to worry about that expense." "Oh, college is coming up in a year for the youngest. That's a big difference."

The Yearly Conversation will help you make future decisions, ahead of time.

I have this same conversation with my dad, so that I know, "Will Mom have to move? Or can she stay in her place? In case I'm the one paying the bills, do you have a budget documented somewhere, so I'll have an idea of what the outgoing is?"

Because really, you're asking somebody to step in and run the business of your life. Even if somebody doesn't want to give you specifics now, you don't have to know how much money they have, but it's good to know, "Oh, there'll be enough money coming in for six months before Mom would have to do something different."

Dead guys can't answer the phone.

Dead guys don't have e-mail.

Dead guys can't advise you.

Start having Yearly Conversations now. Document your recommendations now on the Yearly Conversation Starter Form on the last page of this Drawer. Make sure everyone involved always knows where the Yearly Conversation document is (ideally, with the rest of your Legacy Wardrobe). It's the living guy's guide to survival. It's the dead guy's way to help after he's gone.

It's a conversation I can't imagine anybody regretting they had.

Now do this:

1. Using this chapter as a guide, have your first what-if planning conversation with your spouse, aging parent, or adult child, so you're prepared when one of you becomes a dead guy.
2. Copy the Yearly Conversation Starter Form at the end of this drawer. Or, request a full-size version at www.PrudencePartners.com. (To get the general idea, see the samples at the end of this drawer, after the Yearly Conversation Starter Form.) Document your conversation and financial survival strategies on the Yearly Conversation Starter Form.
3. The what-if conversation is an ongoing conversation. Update your recommendations yearly.
4. Each year put your new Yearly Conversation Starter Form into your Drawer #8 folder. Keep the folder in a secure place.
5. Make sure everyone involved knows where the Drawer #8 folder is kept.

Once you're done, your Legacy Wardrobe Drawer #6 will be in place, so you won't ever have to freak out about your future. It will be there, greatly reducing your angst.

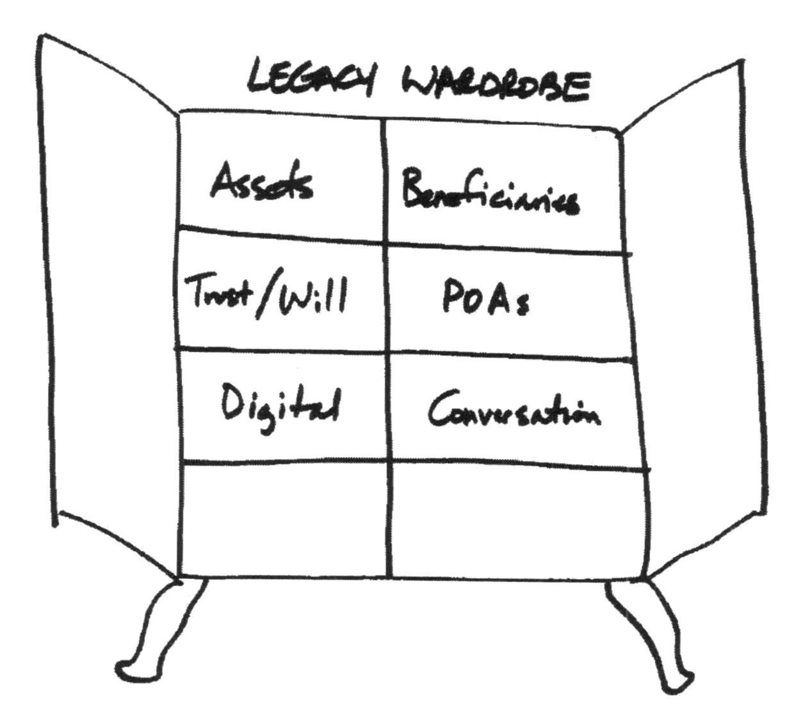

Coming up next: Now that we've wrapped up how to survive a dead guy . . .

- ✓ with a Master List of Assets
- ✓ with correct beneficiaries
- ✓ via a will and trust
- ✓ while avoiding digital lockout
- ✓ with a yearly what-if plan

- ✓ *and* you have your POAs, just in case you're ever an incapacitated not-dead-yet guy,

let's plan Legacy Wardrobe Drawer #7—how to go out with a bang. Let's plan a funeral that's simply to die for!

~ Best Gift Actionable Form 4 ~

Yearly Conversation Starter Form
Year:
If spouse A becomes the dead guy today, projected income is __________ projected expenses are __________
If spouse B becomes the dead guy today, projected income is __________ projected expenses are __________
Thoughts: ________________________________ ________________________________ ________________________________ ________________________________ ________________________________ ________________________________ ________________________________ ________________________________ ________________________________

Your fourth actionable piece of paper is complete! Now on to the fifth and final one!

***Sample* Budget Form**				
Monthly Expenses			Income Sources	
Item	Amount		Source	Amount
Mortgage				
Car 1				
Car 2				
Electricity				
Gas				
Food				
Eating Out				

***Sample* Calendar of Large Expenses**			
Budget Item	Jan	Feb	Mar . . .
Property Taxes			
Home Insurance			
Umbrella			
Car 1 Insurance			
Car 2 Insurance			
Totals			

Excellent progress!
Your Best Gift is almost complete!

Fact: Dead guys can't pick caskets.

Does it really matter?

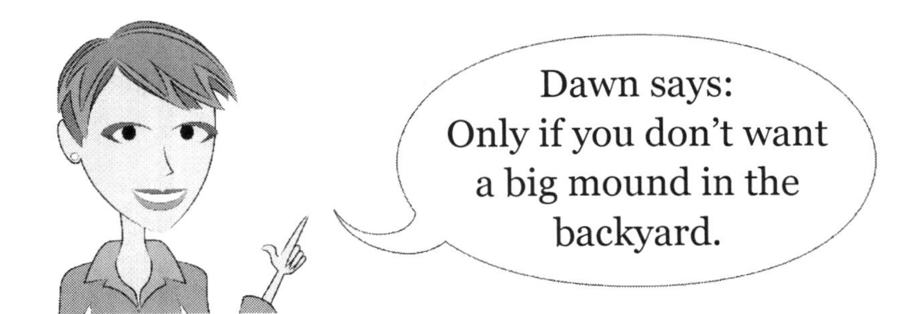

Drawer #7

Skip the Drama

(Funeral Instructions)

Eventually you'll find yourself perfecting your golf stance on a putting green in heaven. Meanwhile, those who admired you in life for your stylishness and your snappy turns of phrase will be pulling items from their wardrobes to attend your last hurrah.

If you're the dead guy, this may seem like no big deal to you, because you're dead. But survivors want to respect your last wishes, as a final way to honor you. And if they don't know what they are, that makes it really hard to figure out.

Maybe in the long run, your funeral service, the going-away party that follows, and which tree they stick you under doesn't really matter that much. But in the moment, it matters a lot to survivors to do something that would have pleased you. It's a burden not to have any direction and to try and figure it out.

Even worse, if it's a group of people, such as a group of siblings, trying to arrange it, now you've just introduced a business element into a relationship that may not work well as group decision makers. And nobody wants that!

So plan and pay for your big send-off yourself, way ahead of time, and save everybody the angst should you suddenly buy it on the eighth hole at Pebble Beach.

That's your Legacy Wardrobe Drawer #7—how to cobble together your funeral instructions.

Wait, you might be thinking, *did you just say I need to pay for my own funeral?* Yep. And if you want to have people get together for lunch to chat about how you were their favorite whatever, that costs money too, to do a regular funeral and luncheon. More if you want to throw a party to remember.

The least expensive cremation alone costs $2000. If you don't pay for it, what that translates into is you telling your children, "Hey, it's going to cost around $12,000 for cremation, funeral, lunch, and probate when I die. If I don't have that money saved up, or if I don't have a trust, you're not going to be able to access any of my money, so I suggest you start saving now, so you can front the money for my death."

If you're pretty sure you're not moving again, and you're older, plan your funeral. Prepay for your funeral. Then you'll be free to focus on your golf swing.

Choices, Choices

If you're going to be placed in a casket like lettuce in a taco shell, do you want an open casket or closed casket (which would be more like a burrito). What are your wishes?

What songs or Scripture passages do you want at the funeral? Poems? Is there anything specific that would be uniquely you and meaningful to everyone there? Who do you want to speak? Who do you want involved, and how? What cards or other mementos do you want guests to be given to keep?

Will you have a celebration-of-life party to follow? Do you want it simple? Do you want it catered? Where will it take place? Do you want a live band playing Dixieland jazz? It's your party. You get to pick.

Do you want to be cremated afterward? What kind of urn would look good wrapped around you?

(If you cremate in a crematory, you save a lot of money compared to paying a funeral home.)

And then where do you want to be buried? Or do you want your ashes scattered someplace? Some people have specific ideas, others don't. If parents leave these decisions to their adult children, that can introduce a problem into the relationship. Some siblings don't talk very often, or even get along very well. And now they're going to insert a business element into their relationship when someone dies, and figure it out together?

Buried or scattered. Does it matter? Actually, it might matter a lot to survivors that they can visit somebody. Some people like their ashes to be scattered in the Pacific or on a mountain. You can't really visit anybody there. So being able to visit might be important to alive guys.

Talk to your family. Have the conversations. Plan and document what gets done with you before you cross the great divide, so that no one needs to plan after. Especially if you don't have money, and you're strapped. There are options. And dead guys can't pick caskets.

We Are Mr. Potato Heads

My husband was an organ donor. That was actually one of the first phone calls I received after he died—from an organ and tissue donation company. This is another disturbing side of death practices, especially if a survivor isn't prepared for it. This is kind of funny, but it's sick, in a grim Mr. Potato Head sort of way. You have to answer all of these gut-wrenching questions to give permission for the harvesting. So anyway, we got through that. Then they came and harvested what they thought would help people, and of course that was before Tom's funeral.

My husband had an open casket, and he looked a little weird. Even with long sleeves, particularly his arms didn't look right. Later I learned it was because they harvested skin from his arms (and his legs, but his legs weren't visible in the casket).

Afterward, they send you a lot of information in the mail. "Thank you so much for helping your loved one. . . ."

Well, on the one-year anniversary of my husband's death, I got a letter in the mail from the organ and tissue organization. And they said, "Thank you again for your husband being willing to be an organ donor. Unfortunately, nothing that we harvested was able to be of any use to anybody."

I thought, *Really? Did you have to send this letter? Did you have to open up that scab again? Do I really need to know this?"* I wonder if there was some ridiculous regulation that made them send that out.

Anyway, the takeaway here is that a live guy's wishes about organ donation is worth a really good conversation. Because people should be prepared for it. "You're going to be an organ donor, great. What does that mean? Does that mean your body might be kept alive for a certain period of time? Does it mean we might have to wait for organs to be harvested before we can say good-bye?"

I talked to a friend of mine about when her father-in-law was dying. When he died, a nurse came in and said, "Okay we're going to take . . ." whatever organ they were going to take. And the man's wife blurts out, "Are you going to cut his head off in front of us?"

Well, they don't cut heads off anyway. But in this moment of extreme emotional vulnerability and angst, it'd be nice to know, "What does that mean that you're going to be an organ donor?" so that it's not shocking. Organ donation is noble and necessary, but not painless for the survivors.

That's an important conversation to have. Always plan to take care of your survivors. Always plan your Legacy Wardrobe, period. Or you might end up as a big mound in someone's backyard.

Now do this:

1. Using this chapter as a guide, plan your last hoorah.
2. Document your wishes using the Funeral Instructions form on last page of this Drawer. Or, request a full-size version at www.PrudencePartners.com. Communicate your wishes with your family.
3. If you're pretty sure you're not moving again, and you're older, pay for your funeral, the party, and the plot where they'll park you. There are even funeral trusts with which you can fund your last hoorah and make funds available.
4. Put your funeral, burial, and related documents into your Legacy Wardrobe Drawer #8 folder. Keep the folder in a secure place.
5. Make sure everyone involved knows where the Drawer #8 folder is kept.

After you've done that, your Legacy Wardrobe Drawer #7 will be accomplished, and whenever you become a dead guy, you'll significantly reduce your family's angst.

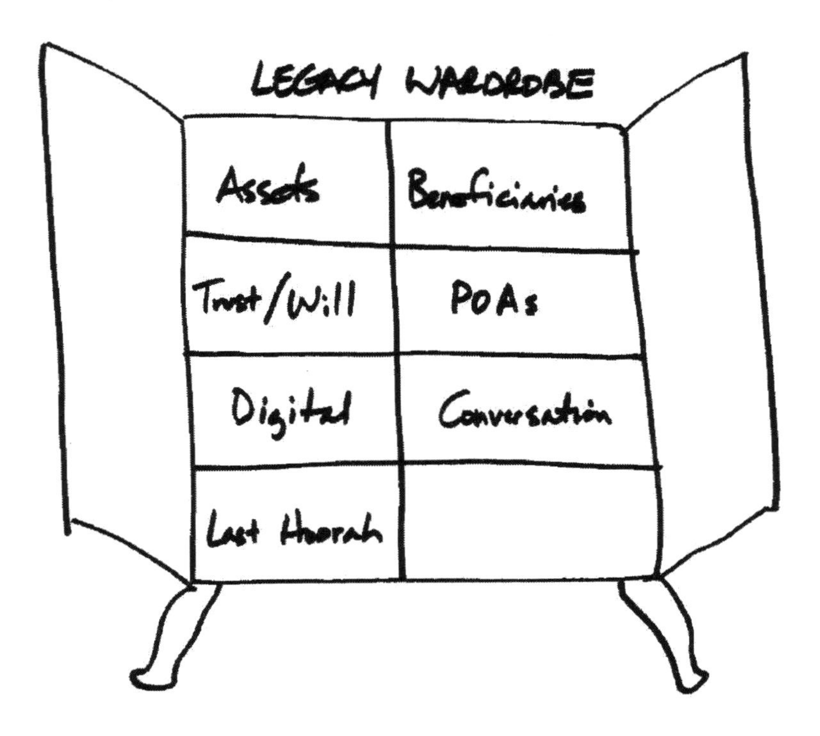

Coming up next: It's the eighth and last drawer in your Legacy Wardrobe, where your Best Gift will be completed . . . and you'll know that you and your family will always be protected!

~ Best Gift Actionable Form 5 ~

Funeral Instructions for Spouse ___________ (name)
I Am/Am Not an Organ Donor (Circle One)
For My Cremation and/or Burial:
For My Funeral Service:
For My Celebration of Life Party:
How to Fund the Expenses:

Your fifth and final actionable Legacy Wardrobe piece of paper is complete! Now on to the last drawer!

Fact: Dead guys can’t make phone calls.

Does it really matter?

Drawer #8

Congratulations!

You Just Wrapped The Best Gift!

Surprise! If you've already completed your Legacy Wardrobe Drawers #1 - #7, then you've already completed Drawer #8! All of your hard work is done!

Drawer #8 is a compilation of the key documents from Drawers #1 - #7. The rest of Drawer #8 is handy bonus materials for survivors when someone becomes a dead guy.

Altogether, it's a simple step-by-step guide of who to call and what to do when an alive guy becomes a dead guy.

Drawer #8 is The Best Gift.

If you're the dead guy, the Best Gift lets your family know what to do. If your spouse is the dead guy, it lets *you* know what to do.

The Best Gift is for the survivor, not for the dead guy. It helps the survivor know how to move forward.

After a death, every transaction is emotionally loaded. It's difficult to remember even the easiest information. That's why we documented every piece of actionable information to put into The Best Gift, so the alive guy doesn't have to hunt, think, or recall, just *do*.

For me, I was clueless for so long. That added a lot of angst, because I didn't know what to do. With The Best Gift, you or your survivor will know what to do.

Now you have just a few more things to gather.

1. Assemble the last seven years of tax returns.
2. Gather certificates/decrees: birth, death, prenuptial agreement, marriage, divorce military.
3. If you have a safe deposit box, list location, authorized users, and the location of the key.

The following items in this numbered list are the five actionable pages from your Legacy Wardrobe Drawers #1 - #7, which you've been assembling into your Drawer #8 folder, your Best Gift. Make certain all of these are in your Best Gift folder.

1. Master List of Assets with beneficiaries.
2. Trust/Will/POA Master List.
3. Master List of User IDs and Passwords.
4. Yearly Conversation Starter Form your Budget Form and Calendar of Large Expenses.
5. Funeral Instructions.

You'll also need a copy of the following, **Steps to Take after a Loss**. Or, request a full-size version at www.PrudencePartners.com.

Steps to Take after a Loss

I am very sorry for your loss. I hope these steps will help you through the difficult days to follow.

1. Use a notebook to keep track of all transactions and communications. There will be many, and they'll be difficult to remember.
2. Call the people on your Trust/Will/POA Master List. Your estate attorney and financial planner will be a great help during this process.
3. You will need death certificates before you can apply for any benefits. I recommend ordering twenty certificates, because ordering additional death certificates after receipt of the initial ones costs more money and takes more time.
4. Someone needs to write an obituary and place it in the local newspaper.
5. You need cash (write a check) to cover cremation/burial and funeral costs, in addition to normal ongoing expenses.
6. Have someone stay at the residence during the wake and funeral to discourage opportunistic looters.
7. Designate a helper to keep track of monies received from sympathy cards so that thank-you notes can be written in a timely fashion. Consider having a helper write them for you.

8. Have someone accompany you to the florist, funeral home, church, etc. Another set of eyes and ears and support are valuable.
9. Assign someone the task of locating and securing a restaurant or church for a meal after the funeral.
10. Contact deceased's place of employment. Find out details about pension, retirement benefits, and life insurance. If there is a pension, now is a good time to find out what the rules are for remarriage. Not that it's on your mind now, but later it will be helpful in assessing future options. Also find out medical insurance coverage costs and rules for remarriage.
11. Contact life insurance companies to request necessary paperwork. Typically benefits will flow within sixty days after receipt of the completed packet, which requires the death certificate.
12. Send a death certificate to each of the three major credit bureaus. It's really important to shut down the deceased's identity to prevent identity theft and fraud. You can request the addresses at www.prudencepartners.com.
13. The trust, will, and POAs for health care and finance will need to be updated.
14. Contact Social Security. You will need to make an appointment to complete paperwork. Also, you will receive $250 to help with funeral costs. No

kidding—Social Security refers to it as a "lump sum." It's just a very small lump.

15. All social media accounts need to be shut down.
16. Take all rewards points from credit cards two weeks prior to notifying them of deceased's death. There are rules governing those points, and the points will be lost if both transactions happen at the same time.
17. Contact the bank to notify them of the deceased's passing.
18. Keep one joint bank account open, so that when you receive checks made out to the dead guy, you may easily deposit them.
19. Contact utilities to change the primary name on the accounts. This takes way more time than you'd anticipate.

Now do this:

1. Copy **Steps to Take after a Loss** or request a full-size version at www.PrudencePartners.com.
2. Put all of your Drawer #8 documents into your Legacy Wardrobe Drawer #8 folder. This folder is now your Best Gift. Keep the folder in a secure place.
3. Make sure everyone involved knows where your Best Gift is kept.

4. Update your Best Gift each year. (Because people move. And phone numbers change.)

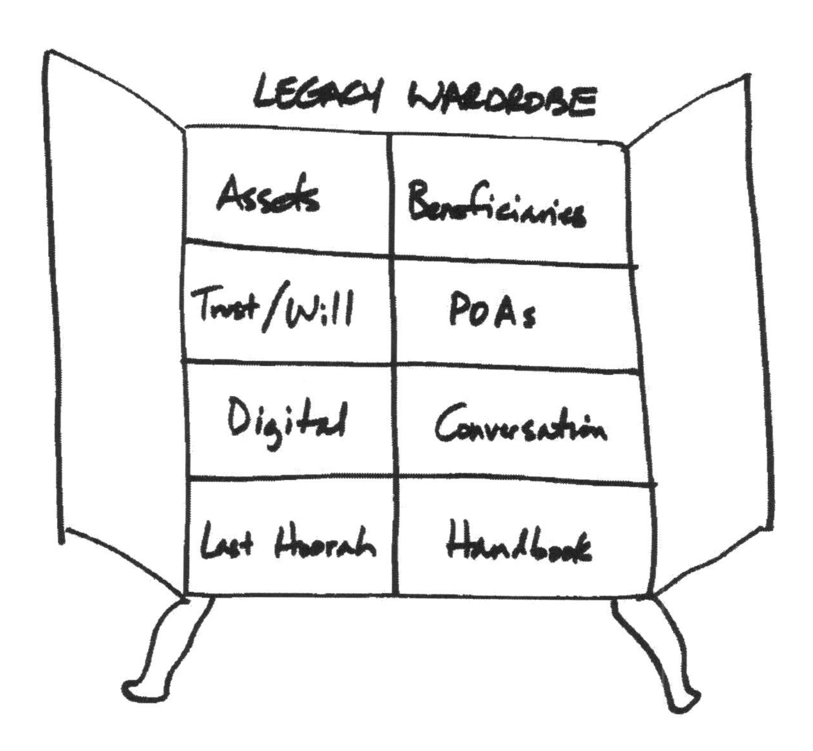

Congratulations! With that, you have finished creating your Best Gift and have eliminated unnecessary angst in life!

Your Legacy Wardrobe, which is your Best Gift, is complete!!! Now you know what's in your drawers. You have all the information you need, at a glance, to easily manage your affairs now and when someone becomes a dead guy.

You will be able to live the rest of your years knowing you have your affairs in order, and you have done so to protect your family relationships.

Remember, The Best Gift is Your Last Gift.

Glossary of Terms

affairs—documents that show what stuff you own and what will happen to the stuff (affairs = documents)

assets—your stuff (assets = stuff)

beneficiary—a person who gets an asset (beneficiary = who gets a dead guy's stuff)

beneficiary audit—reviewing your beneficiary forms every three to five years, or whenever a life change occurs, to be certain they're accurate (audit = review)

beneficiary form—a document that reveals who will inherit an asset (asset = stuff)

executor—the person you appoint to carry out the terms of your will (a female is an executrix) when you become a dead guy

getting your affairs in order—arranging your affairs in such a way that survivors will be able to manage well when you become a dead guy. This includes the legal, financial, and digital aspects of your life.

HIPAA— Health Insurance Portability and Accountability Act

important document—a document that proves you own something or gives instructions. For example, your 401k, IRA, and life insurance each come with a document that shows it's yours. Wills, trusts, and POAs give instructions. (important document = shows ownership or gives instructions)

POA for finance—the person (agent) you designate who will make financial decisions on your behalf, in case you become incapacitated

POA for health care— the person (agent) you designate who will make decisions on your behalf, related to your health care, in case you become incapacitated

probate—court process that supervises the distribution of a dead guy's assets (stuff)

successor executor—the second-string executor in case the executor dies or can't carry out his or her obligations

successor trustee—the person in charge of distributing assets from a trust when the trustee becomes a dead guy

trust—document that describes how your assets will be managed while you're an alive guy, *or* distributed when you become a dead guy, in such a way as to avoid your estate going to probate (court)

trustee—the person in charge of managing or distributing assets from a trust, typically the person who created the trust

will—document that describes how your assets will be distributed when you become a dead guy

About the Author

Dawn Pruchniak suffered the sudden and completely unexpected loss of her husband when she was fifty-four years of age, while their triplets were seniors in high school. Overnight she was thrust into getting all her affairs in order, but had no idea how much work was ahead of her *or* how much more difficult it would make the grieving process.

Dawn quickly realized there were too many things she wasn't living ready for. She learned the hard way that the best time to know what you have, what it means, and what you need is *before* a major life event happens. At a conservative estimate, it took 300 hours to get her affairs in order.

In 2012 Dawn became a Family Affairs Specialist and formed Prudence Partners. Since then, she and her team have been helping others to avoid the same risks she once faced. Her personal experience has led her to her life purpose—to help people **leave their Best Gift**.

A background in engineering and sales is the foundation for her systematic and personal approach to help people organize their affairs so they can create their Best Gift.

Life happens. Dawn makes it easy for people to protect their treasured family relationships and live with confidence so they can enjoy life.

Discover how Dawn can personally help you create your Best Gift at www.TheBestGiftisYourLastGift.com.